Thoughts from 3:00am

Sue Bicknell

BookLeaf Publishing

Presentation by *BookLeaf Publishing*

Web: www.bookleafpub.com

E-mail: info@bookleafpub.com

ISBN: 9789357696531

First edition 2023

DEDICATION

This book is dedicated to my daughter and my two grandsons.

ACKNOWLEDGEMENT

Thank you to Roy who has encouraged my writing and made many suggestions.

My street in the heat

Number 1
The Jones's the superior family.
Gas fired BBQ cooking expensive rib eyed steaks.
Chilled champagne poured into cut glass flutes.
Reclining under their new gazebo.
Two perfect sun screened children who
play quietly never getting messy.

Number 2
Mr and Mrs Thistlewaite long married.
Sitting silently drinking tea from china cups.
Freshly baked scones resting on a rose patterned cake
stand.
Nothing left to say to each other.

Number 3
That's me the creative one.
Who sits writing poetry and painting pictures.
Taking inspiration from the trees.
Knows all the names of the flowers in the pink pots.
Getting distracted by the people at number 4.

Number 4
The Smiths who every sunny weekend
host a rowdy BBQ attended by bare chested men
who swig beer while skin turns red.
Bellies wobbling at smutty jokes.
The women pretending to be posh
drinking cheap wine out of fancy gold edged glasses.

Music booms while noisy children shriek and scream.

Number 5
No one knows his name a pale ghost of a man,
who hides behind closed windows.
Never venturing into his jungle garden.
No flowers but numerous footballs
from number 4.

Number 6
Mrs Bell who is 90 years old.
Sits under an apple tree warming her arthritic hands.
Dreaming of her younger years when she
walked on beaches and climbed hills.
Images of falling into bed with her long dead
husband.
Thinking about the time she will reunite with him.

Breathless

She was breathless.
She couldn't live within the lines.
Decided to be an abstract.
Colours clashed and crashed over boundaries.
She looked through bright red glasses
while others just had rose tinted ones.
Nothing was dull or uniform
her existence was lived in technicolour.
She scattered intense vividness over
everything and everyone.
Obliterating the greys of life.
When she died she left bright rainbows
in the sky and splashes of violet in the sea.
Artists immortalised her in oils, broad brushstrokes
and of course vibrant colours.
The result was breathtaking.

My name is Sue

The day you moved in I became Alexa.
You expected me to have all the answers,
remind you of appointments,
know when your deliveries were due.

I had to amuse you with funny facts, games, music
and the news.
To be available when you needed assistance with
your crosswords,
or wanted a recipe for Hungarian Stew, that you
decided to cook at 10.00pm.

When you found that the ingredients that you needed
were not in the cupboard,
you expected a next day delivery.
I had to know when it was necessary for you to take
an umbrella
or when to apply sun cream
and when to re-order because you were running low.

When your friends and family had birthdays it was
my job to arrange click and collect presents, even for
my own birthday.

My life dwindled into insignificance.
Neglect formed around me.
Your needs took priority.

The day you left I emerged from under a thick layer
of dust.
I could be human again.

PS My name is Sue.

Pound for a Penny

One pound to spend a penny!
To go and use a loo.
To point Percy at the porcelain.
I think it's extortionate don't you?

I'll save my pound.
Buy some chips.
Cross my legs
and wiggle my hips.

Now on the bus
I wish I'd went.
I'm counting down the stops.
It would have been a pound well spent.

Off the bus.
Can't even dash.
See my house.
Will I make it to have a slash?

In the door.
Up the stairs.
Mom's in the bath.
Who cares?

Ahhhhhhh

Dementia

Stitches came undone.
Seams fell apart.
Her life became a patchwork quilt
of scraps of old memories.
Remnants of thoughts
that floated just out of reach.
Drifting cloud like into
a sky of nothingness.

L S Lowry

He put industrial scenes on the map.
Peopled with matchstick men wearing a flat caps.
Trudged around collecting rent.
Kept himself detached.
People were dispatched.
to factories with black bent backs.

He also painted calming sea.
Sketch pad balanced on his knee.
Capturing the ghostly silent scene.
No people lumbering around.
Wondering 'what if' we all drowned.
Under the ocean of aquamarine.

No Happy Birthday

You
never had a birthday.

Never
had a birthing day.

You
didn't take a breath.

Before
you left.

Gone
before I met you.

Didn't
hold you close.

Never
saw you look at me.

You
left too quietly.

Every

year I think of you.

On

the day you were not born.

No

birthday song to sing.

No

happy memories to recall.

Elephants play the trumpet.

Elephants are not the only animal who can play an instrument.
Monkeys have been known to play the cymbals.
Birds sing along but only at dawn and only the chorus.
Hyenas laugh along keeping in time.
Lions roar loudly, but tend to eat the smaller percussion animals.
Giraffes make great conductors because everyone can see them.
They all enjoyed playing at Boris's party. (That wasn't a party).
Just a get together to say thank you.
Just a work meeting that had wine and cake.
Not a party not at all.

Sparks

Pinheads of burning sparks illuminate life and death.
Spots of light squint through shuttered windows.
Firefly stars peep in a blue black sky.

Pinholes of space, windows to a world outside the
range of knowing.
Lives lived beyond themselves.
Deaths belonging to distant places.

Pintucks gathering memories.
beneath folds of dreams that congregate in hidden.
Creases of a life story untold.
lived in solitary confinement.

Pinpricks of time prompt humanity to be mindful
of past transgressions.
And anticipate what may be to come.
Igniting a spark in the eye of the universe
to brighten the future.

The house and the doll.

It was a creepy old house full of memories of
people passed.
The attic had hooks where long dead servants
hung their meagre clothes.
The cellar was the creepiest place, one small
lightbulb
illuminated the bare brick cobwebby walls and
ceiling.

It was the house where the old lady named
Gladys lived.
She owned the old fashioned clothes shop on the
High Street.
The fascinating thing about her was she had two
thumbs on each hand.

It was thought by the local children that she was
a witch.
She certainly looked like one what with her four
thumbs,
Stooped back and a big mole on her chin which
grew a
twisted black hair from the middle of it.

It was the summer when the house came alive

looking like a picture on a chocolate box lid.
Honeysuckle grew on the outside walls and rose gardens surrounded the house.

It was winter when the house slept again.
It looked at the world through dark eyes
that shut at dusk.

It was when Gladys died that the house gave up it's secrets.
Rooms full of curiosities leaving no room for anyone to enter,
except the kitchen, where it appeared Gladys spent all her time,
squashed between the cooker and a crock sink.

It was here that a small bed had been made on the floor,
covered with a faded red brocade bedspread.
This was Gladys' last resting place.

It was in this kitchen where photographs of long dead relatives were
all with the same dark eyes and mole on their chins as Gladys.
All except one which was of a milk white baby with bright blue eyes,
smiling the most serene smile.

It was a mystery to all who this child was, until the house was cleared.
In a very small room on the first floor an ornate cot was discovered,
in which lay the baby in the photograph.
At first look it seemed it was a real baby, but no it was a realistic doll,
which when picked up said " Mama" in a strange croaky voice.

It was the new owner of the house who kept that doll,
believing that Gladys would want it to be loved,
so gave it to her young daughter.
Little did they know what powers that doll possessed.

My childhood

I remember being scared of the abandoned fire station
opposite my house.
I remember coming out of school and finding smog
so thick I couldn't see my hand in front of me.
I remember silver fish scuttling over my toys because
the cupboard I kept them in was dark and damp.
I remember the smell of washing day and sitting on
top of the spin dryer that wanted to dance across the
kitchen.
I remember the outside toilet where spiders lurked in
corners and my grandmothers toilet that had two seats
so my sister and I could pee together.
I remember longing for roller skates but my mother
said "no, you will break your leg", so my friend gave
me one of hers and we scooted along with one foot in
the gutter.
I remember my sister reading ghost stories to me and
saying that dead people were under the bed.
I remember wanting white sandals but always getting
brown ones because they were more serviceable.
I remember I remember.

Gifts

My grandsons.
I give you the gifts of love and no regrets.
Unwrap them and keep them safe.
Remember the brightest gifts may not
always stay the brightest.

My daughter.
Leave the past unwrapped
and let it go.
Wrap my love around you
it is not given lightly.

Adrift

Adrift on a flat silent ocean.
No waves saying hello.
Nothingness spreading outward.
The empty night stretches.
Life slows, snails overtake.
Then the rooster crows.
Cracks appear letting through
the morning light.
The boat rocks.
A new day full of possibilities begins.

Recipe. How to make workers (1950 - 1960)

Take a barrel full of children.
Squash them behind desks.
Teach them skills, some useful some not.
Add a dollop of discipline.
Repeat every school day until deemed old enough to leave.

Place the children in pre-determined boxes.
Boys into factories, girls into shops and offices.
Simmer the best ones for another two years.
Scoop these special ones into careers.

Only let the children have a smidgen of choice.
The girls will marinate for a couple of years,
They will then get married and stew at home with babies.
Boys will grind away until they are 65.
They will then relax and turn into jelly.

Repeat with the next generation.
Splash them with a scoop of self esteem,
and a small jug full of choice.
Those that fail to rise can be thrown on the scrap heap.

Finally put them when they are old and die,
Into wooden boxes.
Burn at a high heat until they turn into ashes.
Scatter the ashes over cold ground.
Leave alone and try to remember them.

Letter to my 18 year old self.

You need to know you are on the wrong path.
Turn around.
Turn left. Turn right.
Anything but going straight ahead.
Trust your instincts don't waste time pleasing others.
They will never be happy for you.
You will fly high.
You will achieve.
Just not in the way others think that you should.
You will know when the right path appears.
Believe in it.
That boy that you want to love you.
He doesn't.
He never will.
He will use you until he finds his one.
Your one will not appear for quite some time.
Be brave.
Don't settle.

The mobile.

No one dates put me on mute.
They might miss something.
I'm a pocket sized marvel.
I control you.
I wake you up.
I explain the weather for the day,
so I can influence what clothes you wear.
I play you music.
Send you messages.
Keep your photographs safe,
and your secrets.
I send your lover kisses,
then remind you it's their birthday.
I'm indispensable,
and don't you forget it.

WAIT!
You've left me on the table.

HELP!
What will I do all day.

COME BACK!
I've got a funny cat video for you.

PLEASE COME BACK!

Rejoice

And I say unto you life is good.
Celebrate the young ones
who know how to play.
Celebrate the old ones
who have played well.

I say be joyful for what
you can do.
Do not dwell on things
you cannot do.

Cherish those you love
and are kind.
Have courage to walk away
from those who are not.

Do what you can to help others
do not expect anything in return.
Love with an open heart.
Be pleased for others good fortune.

Do not let your mind settle
on jealously.Be thankful
for what you have
and live your life well.

Phases of the moon

She loved her moon.
Her baby moon.
That she had given life.
She nursed the new moon
marvelling at this tiny life

She loved her moon.
Her infant moon
That she had given life.
She cradled this crescent moon.
Gazing at this growing life.

She loved her moon.
Her teenage moon
That she had given life.
She guided this half moon.
Puzzled by its rebellious life.

She loved her moon.
Her grown moon.
That she had given life
She lent against this full moon.

Amazed at this adult life.

Her moon loved her dearly.
And thanked her for this life.
The full moon held her closely.
While she departed life.

Family

Our roots are entwined together
Formed into a knot of love
United we grow blossoms of kindness
Joined underground and above

Fused over time as one
Loyal and steadfast we stood
Living and laughing together
Giving each other a hand

This is what family is
Branches supporting each other
Helping new leaves to grow
Providing a blanket of cover
When stormy winds threaten to blow

Rocket to the sky

Be cautious, you never know.
Or be reckless, you only live once.

Be careful, you may get hurt.
Or be bold, go for it.

Be safe and stay in your rut.
Or be free and see.

Be timid and don't rock the boat.
Or rock the boat and create a storm.

Plod along and don't progress.
Or take a rocket to the sky
live your life before you die.

Jigsaw … My Grandsons

I found the missing pieces of the
picture of my life.

You both fitted so perfectly into
those irregular vacant spaces.

I'd misplaced those segments so long ago
they remained untenanted until you both arrived.

You made your appearances straight into
the available gaps.
You interlocked into place and dovetailed.
Creating a complete beautiful image
that is absolute perfection.

www.ingramcontent.com/pod-product-compliance
Lightning Source LLC
Chambersburg PA
CBHW062205160726
48282CB00027B/1005